THE STORY OF THE
LOS ANGELES LAKERS

THE NBA: A HISTORY OF HOOPS

THE STORY OF THE
LOS ANGELES LAKERS

SHANE FREDERICK

CREATIVE EDUCATION

Published by Creative Education
P.O. Box 227, Mankato, Minnesota 56002
Creative Education is an imprint of The Creative Company
www.thecreativecompany.us

Design and production by Blue Design
Art direction by Rita Marshall
Printed in the United States of America

Photographs by Alamy (Russell Kord), Basketballphoto
.com (Steve Lipofsky), Corbis (Jeff Lewis/Icon SMI), Getty
Images (Andrew D. Bernstein/NBAE, Walter Bibikow,
Kevork Djansezian, James Drake/Sports Illustrated, Noah
Graham/NBAE, George Long/Sports Illustrated, NBAE
Photos/NBAE, NBAP/NBAE, Mike Powell/Allsport, Wen
Roberts/NBAE), Newscom (FREDERIC J. BROWN/
AFP, Icon Sports Media 592/Icon Sports Media, John W.
McDonough/Icon SMI, Jim Ruymen/UPI Photo Service),
USA TODAY Sports (Manny Rubio)

Library of Congress Cataloging-in-Publication Data
Frederick, Shane.
The story of Los Angeles Lakers / Shane Frederick.
p. cm. — (The NBA: a history of hoops)
Includes index.
Summary: An informative narration of the Los Angeles
Lakers professional basketball team's history from its 1947
founding in Minneapolis, Minnesota, to today, spotlighting
memorable players and events.
ISBN 978-1-60818-434-7
1. Los Angeles Lakers (Basketball team)—History—Juvenile
literature. I. Title.

GV885.52.L67F73 2014
796.323'640979494—dc23   2013038290

CCSS: RI.5.1, 2, 3, 8; RH.6-8.4, 5, 7

First Edition
9 8 7 6 5 4 3 2 1

Cover: Guard Kobe Bryant
Page 2: Center Pau Gasol
Pages 4&5: Guard Michael Cooper
Page 6: Guard Kobe Bryant

TABLE OF CONTENTS

COURTSIDE STORIES

INTRODUCING...

LAND OF
10,000 LAKERS

GRIFFITH OBSERVATORY OFFERS VIEWS OF LOS ANGELES'S SPRAWLING CITYSCAPE.

Los Angeles, California, is known as the "Entertainment Capital of the World." In the early 20th century, a section of the city called Hollywood became the center of the motion picture industry, and it continues to be the place where the majority of movies and TV shows are made. Many of the celebrities who live and work there have been honored with shimmering stars laid in the sidewalks of Hollywood Boulevard. Sports are an important part of L.A.'s entertainment culture, too, and the Los Angeles Lakers of the National Basketball Association (NBA) have always known how to put on a good show.

The Lakers moved to California in 1960, 13 years after the team was formed more than 1,500 miles away in Minneapolis, Minnesota. Two Minnesota businessmen purchased the assets of the Detroit Gems, a struggling National Basketball League (NBL) team, for $15,000 in

1947. They renamed it the Minneapolis Lakers as a nod to the state's fabled 10,000 lakes. But because the players on the Gems' roster had been released from their contracts, the Lakers started out with nothing more than a pile of used equipment and old uniforms.

Thanks to the Gems' last-place finish the previous season, the Lakers had the first pick in a special draft of players made available from the shortlived Professional Basketball League of America. They used the pick to grab George Mikan, a dominant 6-foot-10 center. Under the direction of 31-year-old head coach John Kundla, Mikan and star forward Jim "The Kangaroo Kid" Pollard led the Lakers to a 43–17 record and the NBL championship in 1948.

The Lakers switched to the bigger, more established Basketball Association of America (BAA) in 1948 and continued to wield control over that league as well. They won the 1949 BAA championship, and Mikan, nicknamed "Mr. Basketball," quickly gained recognition as a star. "George glorified in that 'I am number one' feeling," Pollard said. "That's why he was so successful. He wanted to be number one."

When the BAA merged with the NBL to form the NBA for the 1949–50 season, the Lakers went along with the tide, adding powerful

SIGNED BY A SPORTSWRITER

Sid Hartman was a young sports reporter for the *Minneapolis Tribune* in 1947. He was a faithful fan of the local college team, the University of Minnesota Gophers, but he desperately wanted his town to have a professional basketball presence as well. First, he encouraged businessmen Ben Berger and Morris Chalfen to buy the Detroit Gems and move them to Minneapolis. Then he offered a suggestion for the team's name—the Lakers, in honor of the state's 10,000 lakes—and helped recruit players for the team. He surprised everyone by helping sign Stanford University standout Jim Pollard, the team's first forward. And he went above and beyond the call of duty to ink the tall and talented George Mikan as the team's center. Hartman had been asked to drive Mikan to the airport for his return flight to Chicago following an interview, but Hartman didn't want to let Mikan leave without signing with the Lakers. "I made sure to get lost on the way," Hartman later said. "I drove north, rather than south toward the airport." It worked: Mikan missed his flight and signed with the Lakers for $12,000.

INTRODUCING...

GEORGE MIKAN

POSITION CENTER
HEIGHT 6-FOOT-10
LAKERS SEASONS
1948–54, 1955–56

The basketball coach at the University of Notre Dame told George Mikan (#99) that he was too tall, too awkward, and too blind (he wore glasses that were a quarter-inch thick) to play college basketball. But even that demoralizing assessment could not keep Mikan off the court. Chicago's DePaul University was happy to have the towering center, as were the owners of the Professional Basketball League of America's Chicago American Gears, who signed Mikan to a 5-year contract worth $62,000 in 1946. When that team folded one year later, the Minneapolis Lakers were thrilled to snag him. By then, no one considered Mikan clumsy or worried about his eyesight, and his height was his greatest advantage. Mikan scored 10,156 points and grabbed 4,167 rebounds during his 7-year professional career; he even developed an ambidextrous hook shot that allowed him to shoot over shorter defenders. "Mikan had a tremendous, total confidence that he could get the job done," said Lakers forward Vern Mikkelsen. Mikan left the Lakers for good in 1956 and later played a key role in launching the Minnesota Timberwolves, the next NBA team to call Minneapolis home.

forward Vern Mikkelsen and masterful guard Slater Martin. With a versatile roster that also included former University of Minnesota standout guard Whitey Skoog, the Lakers won the league championship in four of their first five seasons in the NBA.

he Lakers were so dominant during the early years of the NBA that new rules were written to make the game more challenging. Some regulations, such as raising the height of the basket, didn't stick. But others, including the 1954 establishment of the 24-second shot clock, are still in effect today. Such constraints, plus the constant double-teaming and fouling that Mikan experienced, took the fun out of the game for him. After the Lakers went 46–26 and won the NBA title in 1954, Mikan retired, though he would return briefly during the 1955–56 season. By then, Pollard had also left the game.

Soon, the team's reign over the Western Division began to slip, and fan attendance dwindled. The Lakers finished last in the league with a miserable 19–53 record in 1957–58. The franchise's original owners were in financial trouble, so before the 1958–59 season, they

sold the club to a group of investors led by Bob Short, owner of a local trucking business. The Lakers lucked out by receiving the first pick in the NBA Draft. Short's choice was forward Elgin Baylor, a shooting star from Seattle University whose flashy playing style was just what the struggling Lakers needed. "If he had turned me down then, I'd have been out of business," Short said later about Baylor. "The club would have been bankrupt."

Baylor saved the team by scoring 24.9 points per game during the 1958–59 season and by helping lead the resurgent Lakers back to the NBA Finals. Unfortunately, they were swept by the mighty Boston Celtics, and for disappointed fans, even Baylor's All-Star performance the next season wasn't enough to keep them interested. As financial woes mounted, Short decided to take the Lakers west, to the city of Los Angeles.

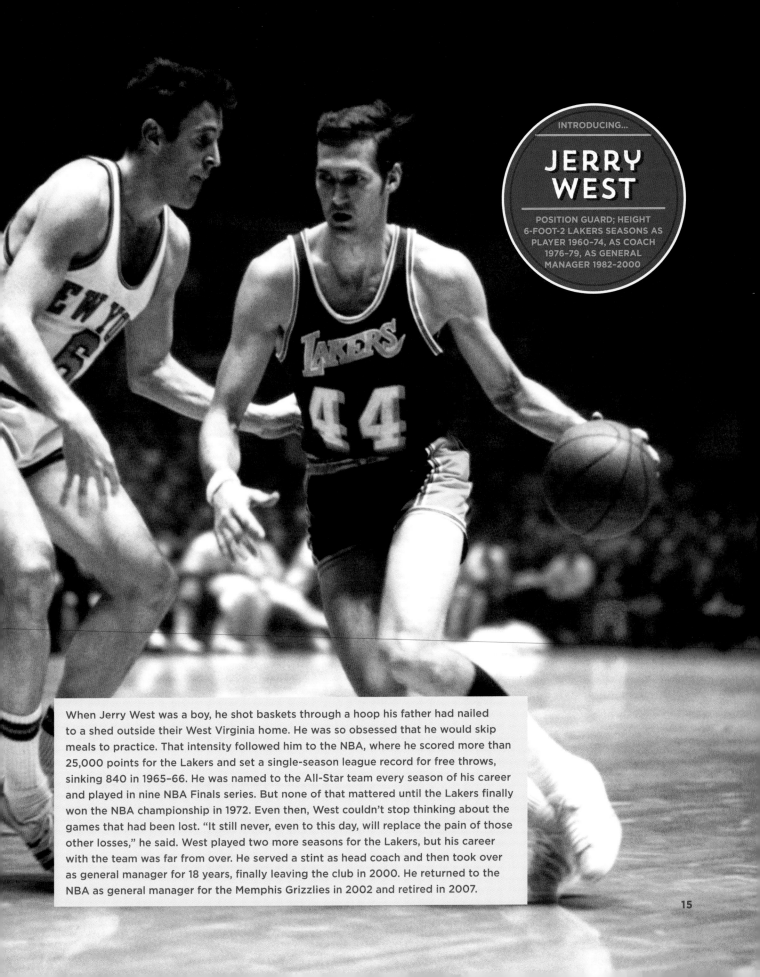

JERRY WEST

When Jerry West was a boy, he shot baskets through a hoop his father had nailed to a shed outside their West Virginia home. He was so obsessed that he would skip meals to practice. That intensity followed him to the NBA, where he scored more than 25,000 points for the Lakers and set a single-season league record for free throws, sinking 840 in 1965–66. He was named to the All-Star team every season of his career and played in nine NBA Finals series. But none of that mattered until the Lakers finally won the NBA championship in 1972. Even then, West couldn't stop thinking about the games that had been lost. "It still never, even to this day, will replace the pain of those other losses," he said. West played two more seasons for the Lakers, but his career with the team was far from over. He served a stint as head coach and then took over as general manager for 18 years, finally leaving the club in 2000. He returned to the NBA as general manager for the Memphis Grizzlies in 2002 and retired in 2007.

15

GO WEST

JERRY WEST MADE UP FOR HIS SMALL SIZE WITH A FEROCIOUS DETERMINATION TO WIN.

The Lakers' arrival in California coincided with that of slender guard Jerry West, who had been drafted out of West Virginia University. Although West was a country kid—Baylor nicknamed him "Zeke from Cabin Creek"—he quickly became a big-city star. In his first professional season, West averaged 17.6 points per game and combined with Baylor to form one of the most dominating backcourt duos in the game.

West and Baylor, along with guard Rodney "Hot Rod" Hundley, led the Lakers to a second-place finish in the Western Division in 1960–61. They improved upon that the following year, clinching the division title with a 54–26 record and cruising into the playoffs.

West earned a new nickname when the Lakers took on the Celtics in the Finals. After scoring twice in the final minute to tie Game 3, he intercepted a pass and, with three

INTRODUCING...

ELGIN BAYLOR

POSITION FORWARD
HEIGHT 6-FOOT-5
LAKERS SEASONS
1958–72

In the world of professional basketball, Elgin Baylor's height never made headlines. But although he stood more than half a foot shorter than his tallest teammates, Baylor played like a big man. He loved to leap up and over opponents, and his hanging jump shots were a favorite with fans in both Minneapolis and Los Angeles. But it wasn't all for show. Baylor set a league record when he single-handedly scored 71 points in a game against the New York Knicks in 1960 (that record was surpassed by Wilt Chamberlain 2 years later), and he tallied more than 23,000 points during his career. Baylor also snared a total of 11,463 rebounds, but it was the points he scored—and the way he scored them—that fans remember most. "He was one of the most spectacular shooters the game has ever known," Lakers guard Jerry West said. "I hear people talking about forwards today, and I haven't seen many that can compare with him."

seconds left on the clock, soared in for the game-winning layup. Suddenly, he was known as "Mr. Clutch." Both the nickname and the memory of that game stayed with him for the rest of his career. "I've never forgotten that," West said. "Everyone wants to hit a home run in the ninth inning to win the big game. That was my home run."

The Lakers won that game but lost the series to the Celtics and repeated that sad scenario five more times in the 1960s. Each time the Lakers—packed with such scoring machines as Baylor, West, and All-Star forward Rudy LaRusso—won the Western Division, they faced the formidable Celtics in the Finals. And each time (in 1963, 1965, 1966, 1968, and 1969), Boston and its star center, Bill Russell, kept Los Angeles from claiming the championship crown.

New owner Jack Kent Cooke tried to reverse that trend in 1968 by trading for Wilt Chamberlain, a 7-foot-1 center who had carried the Philadelphia 76ers to an NBA title in 1967. His presence under the boards helped the Lakers make it back to the Finals in 1969 and 1970. Both times, however, Los Angeles lost in hard-fought, seven-game battles.

After losing to the eventual league champion Milwaukee Bucks in the second round of the 1971 Western Conference playoffs, the Lakers looked as though they were on their way down. But then new coach Bill Sharman instituted intense morning practices and daily running drills. Jim McMillian replaced the retiring Baylor at forward, and guards Gail Goodrich and Pat Riley stepped up as stars. The reinvigorated Lakers won 69 regular-season games in 1971–72, including an NBA-record 33 in a row.

When the Lakers made it to the Finals versus the New York Knicks, they were determined to not lose again. But Game 1, played in Los Angeles, was a disappointment. Fans started filing out of the Forum—the Lakers' home since it opened 1967—early in the second half as the Lakers fell behind and lost, 114–92. But Los Angeles dominated the rest of the series, and with a 114–100 victory in Game 5, the Lakers finally became champions. The tired but jubilant players celebrated in the locker room afterward, and Cooke joined them. "I am very, very, very happy," he said.

It was difficult for a roster of aging stars to sustain that happiness for long, though. The Lakers rallied to return to the Finals against the Knicks the following season but eked out only one win in the humbling five-game series. Chamberlain retired before the 1973–74 season, and West left a year later. After posting a disappointing 30–52 record in 1974–75, the Lakers went looking for a new leader.

STREAKING TO THE TITLE

The Lakers limped through the 1971 playoffs, losing a quick five-game series to the Milwaukee Bucks. So nobody expected the same team to come out swinging the next season. But under new head coach Bill Sharman, that's exactly what Los Angeles did. On November 5, the team had a promising 6–3 record—but Sharman insisted that wasn't good enough. So his team embarked on a 33-game winning streak that is still unmatched in NBA history. The Bucks, who had put together a 20-game streak the previous season, finally ended the Lakers' luck with a 120–104 rout on January 9, 1972. "We knew it had to end sometime," Sharman conceded. But the team soon secured its destiny by posting a 69–13 regular-season record that remained the best in the league until the Chicago Bulls won 72 games in 1995–96. The Lakers went on to capture their fifth NBA championship by defeating the Knicks in the Finals. The exciting path to that title remained unparalleled for team owner Jack Kent Cooke. "It was one of the happiest times in my life," he said.

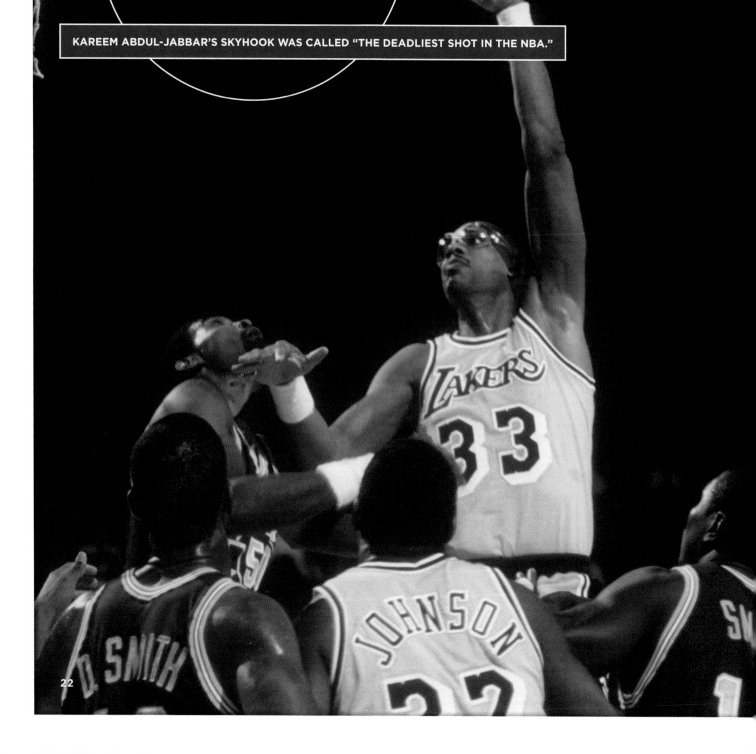

IT'S SHOWTIME

KAREEM ABDUL-JABBAR'S SKYHOOK WAS CALLED "THE DEADLIEST SHOT IN THE NBA."

os Angeles found its next big star in
Milwaukee, Wisconsin: towering center
Kareem Abdul-Jabbar, who had already
won three NBA Most Valuable Player (MVP)
awards with the Bucks. In 1975–76, his first
season with the Lakers, Abdul-Jabbar won
a fourth MVP trophy—becoming the first Lakers player
ever to garner that honor. But despite his tremendous play
and a sterling 30–11 record at home, the Lakers posted a
disappointing 40–42 record overall and failed to qualify for
the playoffs for the second season in a row.

Abdul-Jabbar and his supporting cast didn't let that
happen again. The Lakers improved to 53–29 in 1976–77,
good for first place in the Western Conference's Pacific
Division (which had been formed in 1970) and a return
to postseason play. But the team's dreams of another
championship were derailed by the Portland Trail Blazers in

COURTSIDE STORIES

LAKERS LANGUAGE

Between 1965 and 2001, Chick Hearn announced 3,338 consecutive Los Angeles Lakers home games. His voice became the team's voice, and his words became the team's language. Besides coining several nicknames for Lakers players—"Captain" for center Kareem Abdul-Jabbar, "Nick the Quick" for guard Nick Van Exel, and "The Kid" for guard Kobe Bryant—he introduced countless "Chickisms" to the basketball vocabulary: "air ball," for a shot that misses the hoop entirely; "boo-birds," for fans who booed their own teams; even "slam dunk," which Hearn used frequently while broadcasting during center Wilt Chamberlain's playing days. He called his colorful, descriptive language a "word's-eye view" of the game. Fans and players alike loved to listen to him describe the obvious outcome of a contest: "The game is in the refrigerator, the door is closed, the light is out, the eggs are cooling, the butter is getting hard, and the Jell-O is jiggling." Health concerns forced Hearn's retirement in 2001, but he returned for a farewell ovation from the fans in 2002. Just a few months later, Hearn died.

the second round of the playoffs. Similar stories played out in each of the next two seasons, as the Lakers easily qualified for the playoffs but were eliminated early both times.

The key piece to the Lakers' championship puzzle was picked up in the 1979 NBA Draft, when Los Angeles used the first overall pick on 6-foot-8 guard Earvin "Magic" Johnson. Johnson was tall and strong enough to play forward or center, but he was also a brilliant passer, ball handler, and leader. With Johnson running the point, the Lakers cruised through the 1979–80 season with a 60–22 record and

roared into the NBA Finals, where they met the title-hungry 76ers and their superstar forward, Julius "Dr. J" Erving.

Los Angeles was one win away from the championship when Abdul-Jabbar sprained his ankle and was forced to sit out Game 6. The 20-year-old Johnson then took over, playing at every position and leading Los Angeles to a convincing victory. His monster performance earned Johnson the Finals MVP trophy, but the rookie didn't forget about Abdul-Jabbar. "I know your ankle hurts, Kareem," Johnson joked, "but why don't you get up and dance, anyway?"

HALL-OF-FAMER ABDUL-JABBAR LED ALL NBA SCORERS WITH 38,387 CAREER POINTS AS OF 2014.

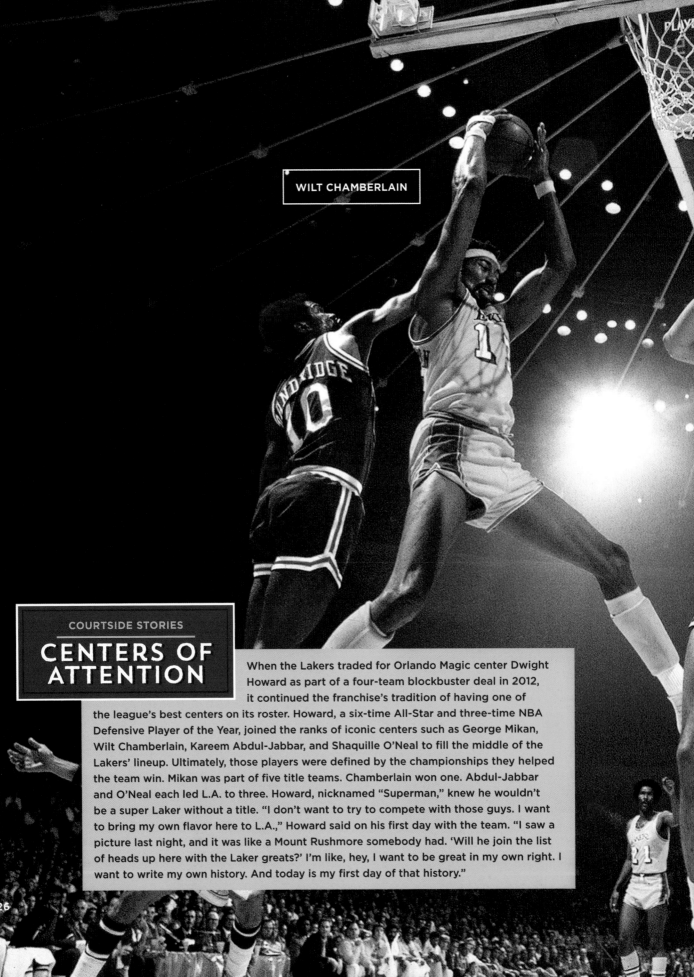

WILT CHAMBERLAIN

CENTERS OF ATTENTION

When the Lakers traded for Orlando Magic center Dwight Howard as part of a four-team blockbuster deal in 2012, it continued the franchise's tradition of having one of the league's best centers on its roster. Howard, a six-time All-Star and three-time NBA Defensive Player of the Year, joined the ranks of iconic centers such as George Mikan, Wilt Chamberlain, Kareem Abdul-Jabbar, and Shaquille O'Neal to fill the middle of the Lakers' lineup. Ultimately, those players were defined by the championships they helped the team win. Mikan was part of five title teams. Chamberlain won one. Abdul-Jabbar and O'Neal each led L.A. to three. Howard, nicknamed "Superman," knew he wouldn't be a super Laker without a title. "I don't want to try to compete with those guys. I want to bring my own flavor here to L.A.," Howard said on his first day with the team. "I saw a picture last night, and it was like a Mount Rushmore somebody had. 'Will he join the list of heads up here with the Laker greats?' I'm like, hey, I want to be great in my own right. I want to write my own history. And today is my first day of that history."

27

Hopes of a repeat the following season were dashed when Johnson was sidelined with torn cartilage in his knee for 45 games. Although Abdul-Jabbar, forward Jamaal "Silk" Wilkes, and hardworking backup guard Michael Cooper led the Lakers back to the playoffs, the Houston Rockets blasted them out in the first round.

Johnson was back at full strength for the 1981–82 season—and just in time. The Lakers hired former guard Pat Riley, a key member of Los Angeles's 1972 championship team, as head coach early in the season. Riley pushed his players hard, but the end result was worth it. Los Angeles compiled an impressive 57–25 record and returned to the NBA Finals, again finding itself up against the 76ers. It took another Game 6 victory to clinch the 1982 championship, but Wilkes put the game away with a beautiful breakaway layup late in the fourth period, and the Lakers won handily, 114–104.

Los Angeles added graceful forward James Worthy in 1982 and athletic guard Byron Scott in 1983. Following the 1984–85 season, the Lakers met their longtime rivals, the Celtics, in the NBA Finals. The Lakers were crushed 148–114 in Game 1, but they battled back and defeated the Celtics in six games—their first Finals win in nine tries against Boston. "It is very sweet," Riley said. "Lakers fans have been waiting for this one a long time."

The Lakers again went on to beat the Celtics in the Finals after the 1986–87 season, prompting Coach Riley to publicly guarantee a repeat the following season. Thanks to Scott's solid shooting and forward A. C. Green's resilient defense, the Lakers made good on Riley's prediction, topping the Detroit Pistons for the 1988 championship crown. But after falling to Detroit in the 1989 NBA Finals, Abdul-Jabbar ended his 20-year playing career. In 1990, Riley stepped down as head coach. The team then sputtered in the 1991 Finals, losing to the Chicago Bulls and their future guard, Michael Jordan.

MAGIC JOHNSON

**POSITION GUARD / FORWARD
HEIGHT 6-FOOT-8
LAKERS SEASONS
1979–91, 1995–96**

Magic Johnson's real name was Earvin, but he was known almost exclusively by his nickname since his days as a high school basketball star. His supernatural skills on the court—from passing and shooting to blocking and rebounding—inspired a sportswriter in Johnson's hometown of Lansing, Michigan, to give him the nickname, and Johnson lived up to it for the rest of his life. When Lakers coach Paul Westhead asked Johnson to step in at center for the injured Kareem Abdul-Jabbar in Game 6 of the 1980 NBA Finals, the rookie replied, "No problem." Johnson scored 42 points in that game, sank 14 free throws, snared 15 rebounds, and dished out 7 assists as the Lakers won the game and the championship. Johnson's "magic" was enhanced by his ear-to-ear grin, which charmed thousands of fans. Although those fans were saddened when Johnson announced that he had tested positive for HIV at a press conference in November 1991, most were inspired by his honesty and courage—including the president of the United States, George H. W. Bush. "For me, Magic is a hero, a hero for anyone who loves sports," Bush said.

REBUILDING THE LAKERS

"BIG GAME" JAMES WORTHY CUT TO THE HOOP FOR SPECTACULAR POSTSEASON PLAYS.

The disappointing end to the 1990–91 season couldn't compare with the devastating loss the team would suffer early on in 1991–92. In November, three-time NBA MVP Magic Johnson tearfully announced that he had tested positive for HIV, that he was retiring immediately, and that he was going to be a spokesperson for those with the virus. "Here I am saying that it can happen to anybody," he said at his press conference. "Even me, Magic Johnson."

The Lakers soldiered on without Johnson, relying heavily on the talents of journeyman guard Sedale Threatt and lanky center Sam Perkins to secure a place in the 1992 playoffs. But Portland quickly eliminated Los Angeles. The same fate befell the team the following season. Then, in 1993–94, the Lakers won only 33 games and missed the playoffs for the first time in 17 seasons.

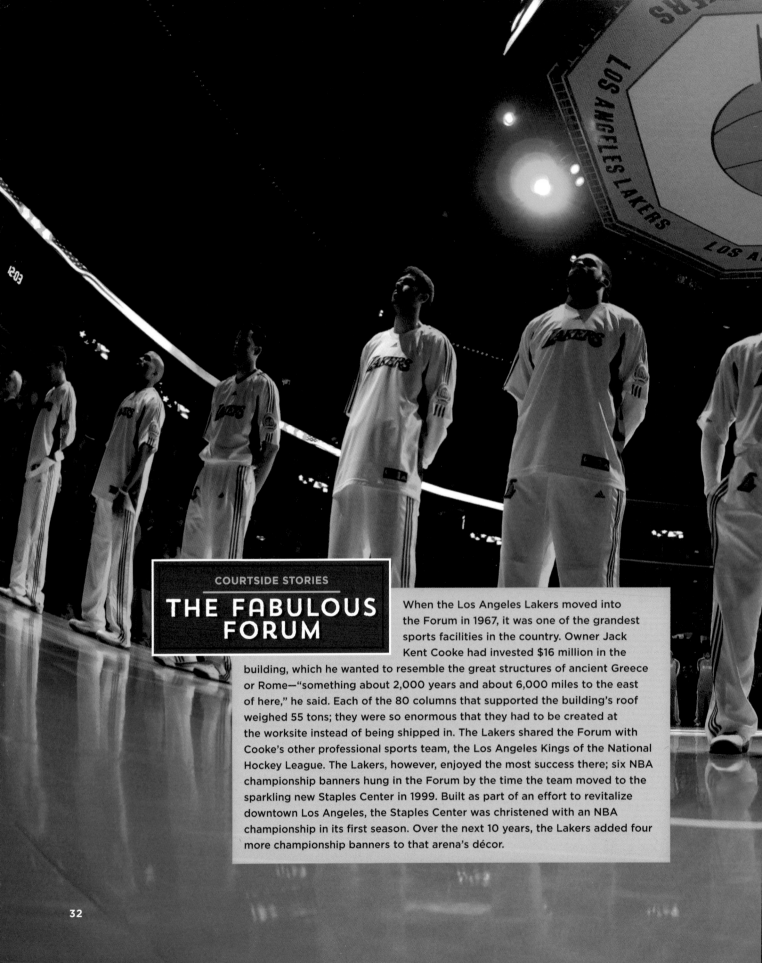

THE FABULOUS FORUM

When the Los Angeles Lakers moved into the Forum in 1967, it was one of the grandest sports facilities in the country. Owner Jack Kent Cooke had invested $16 million in the building, which he wanted to resemble the great structures of ancient Greece or Rome—"something about 2,000 years and about 6,000 miles to the east of here," he said. Each of the 80 columns that supported the building's roof weighed 55 tons; they were so enormous that they had to be created at the worksite instead of being shipped in. The Lakers shared the Forum with Cooke's other professional sports team, the Los Angeles Kings of the National Hockey League. The Lakers, however, enjoyed the most success there; six NBA championship banners hung in the Forum by the time the team moved to the sparkling new Staples Center in 1999. Built as part of an effort to revitalize downtown Los Angeles, the Staples Center was christened with an NBA championship in its first season. Over the next 10 years, the Lakers added four more championship banners to that arena's décor.

However, fiery young guard Nick Van Exel pushed the team to a 48–34 record and a return to the playoffs in 1995. Magic Johnson's comeback for the second half of the following season helped, too, propelling the Lakers to the playoffs again. Johnson retired for good after Los Angeles was eliminated in the first round, making room for another larger-than-life star to assume the spotlight: Shaquille O'Neal, a 7-foot-1 center, was signed before the start of the 1996–97 season. Another pivotal player, guard Kobe Bryant, arrived at the same time. Bryant, an electrifying high school standout from Pennsylvania, had skipped college to enter the NBA Draft. "We've made these moves to prepare for championships

SHAQUILLE O'NEAL

POSITION CENTER
HEIGHT 7-FOOT-1
LAKERS SEASONS
1996–2004

Everything about Shaquille O'Neal was big, from his size 23 shoes to the 7-year, $120-million contract he signed with the Lakers in 1996. (His annual salary of $17 million was more than team owner Jerry Buss paid for the entire team in 1979.) "Shaq" was larger than life, both on and off the court. His sheer strength shattered at least three backboards during the course of his career, and his big body frequently bumped smaller players to the floor during games. His enormous presence down low and strong shooting (with the exception of free throws) helped lead the Lakers to three consecutive NBA championships before he left the team in 2004. O'Neal also recorded five rap albums, launched an acting career, wrote an autobiography, and provided colorful quotes to almost any reporter willing to listen. The big star even liked to talk big. "I know how to win," O'Neal once boasted. "I've been winning all my life, from Little League on. I've never, ever played on a losing team.... I know what it takes to win."

"GUYS HAVE TO FIND OUT WHAT'S IMPORTANT TO THEM. IF THEY DON'T WANT TO PLAY, THEN GET OFF MY TEAM."

— SHAQUILLE O'NEAL ON HIS TEAMMATES' PERCEIVED LACK OF EFFORT

in the present and in the future," said Lakers general manager Jerry West.

Although both players had an impact almost immediately—O'Neal scored 26.2 points per game and was honored as an All-Star, and Bryant's performance off the bench earned him a spot on the NBA All-Rookie team—the championships didn't materialize as quickly. In 1996–97, the Lakers finished second in the Pacific Division but couldn't get past the second round of the playoffs.

os Angeles had a better regular season the next year, winning 61 games and sending 4 players, including the much-matured Bryant, to the All-Star Game. But tension on the team—between players and coach Del Harris—proved to be too much to overcome in the postseason, as the Lakers were swept in the Western Conference finals by the Utah Jazz. O'Neal was so disappointed by what he perceived as his teammates' lack of effort that he lashed out when the series ended. "Guys have to find out what's important to them," he told reporters. "If they don't want to play, then get off my team."

O'Neal's words were prophetic. Van Exel, whose confrontational attitude had rubbed both teammates and coaches the wrong way, was gone before the strike-shortened 1998–99 season. When Coach Harris was dismissed, the Lakers prepared to retool their team for a brighter future.

A NEW
DYNASTY

COACH PHIL JACKSON'S TEAMWORK-BASED PHILOSOPHY MADE FOR A CHAMPIONSHIP SQUAD.

Phil Jackson, who had won six titles in the 1990s as coach of the dominant Bulls, filled the Lakers' head coach vacancy in 1999. Although Jackson's tactics were somewhat unorthodox—among other things, he was known to beat a set of drums on game days to stir up his players—they were successful. The Lakers won 31 of their first 36 games and finished the season 67–15. After earning convincing playoff wins over the Sacramento Kings and the Phoenix Suns, they rallied to defeat the Trail Blazers in a seven-game series that sent them to the 2000 NBA Finals, where they faced the Indiana Pacers.

Both Bryant and forward Robert Horry contributed significantly to Los Angeles's victories in Games 1, 2, 4, and 6, but it was O'Neal's 41-point performance in Game 6 that finally secured an 11th NBA title for the Lakers. "This is why I came here," proclaimed O'Neal. "I wanted to be a champion."

FORWARD RON ARTEST LIKENED HIS OWN STELLAR DEFENSE TO A BOXER'S QUICK JABS.

But one championship was not enough. Although the Lakers recorded fewer regular-season wins in 2000–01, they piled up victories even more quickly in the postseason, sweeping their opponents in the first three rounds of the playoffs before facing the 76ers in the Finals, where they dominated four games to one. For the second consecutive year, O'Neal was named Finals MVP.

When the Lakers "three-peated" by defeating the New Jersey Nets in the 2002 NBA Finals, Los Angeles looked to be on the verge of a long-lasting dynasty. But all was not well in Lakerland, as the team's two biggest stars, O'Neal and Bryant, bickered. The Lakers brought in two veteran players—forward Karl Malone and point guard Gary Payton—in 2003 and reached the Finals in 2004, but the overconfident team lost to the Pistons in an embarrassing five-game series.

That led to the end of an era for the Lakers—O'Neal was traded to the Miami Heat, and Coach Jackson left. Although Bryant remained the team's floor general, he and his new cast of teammates couldn't create any chemistry on the court. Los Angeles went 34–48 in 2004–05 and missed the playoffs for the first time in 11 seasons. The good news was that their poor finish gave the Lakers a better position in the 2005 NBA Draft. Los Angeles selected 7-foot-

KOBE BRYANT

**POSITION GUARD
HEIGHT 6-FOOT-6
LAKERS SEASONS
1996–PRESENT**

Kobe Bryant had not yet celebrated his 18th birthday when he signed his first professional contract in 1996—he was not even old enough to legally sign the papers on his own. Lakers general manager Jerry West was admittedly skeptical about putting a teenager on the team, but he changed his mind after watching Bryant play. "This guy's special," West said. Bryant, who turned 18 before the season started and became the youngest player ever to start in an NBA game, quickly silenced any critics who had doubted that he was ready for the pros. By the time "The Kid" turned 21, he was averaging more than 22 points per game and leading his team to the first of 3 consecutive NBA championships. In 2006–07, when he was 28, he scored 81 points in a game against the Toronto Raptors—the second-highest total for a single game in NBA history. An NBA scout once said of a young Bryant, "The sky is the limit." By 2014, Bryant owned five championship rings and remained just the fifth player in NBA history to reach beyond the 30,000-point milestone.

CENTER ANDREW BYNUM WAS THE YOUNGEST (18 YEARS, 6 DAYS) EVER TO PLAY IN AN NBA GAME.

FAMOUS FANS

The Lakers moved from Minneapolis to Los Angeles in hopes that they would find more fans. In the process, they attracted numerous celebrity spectators as well. One of the team's first famous fans was Doris Day, a singer and actress who sat courtside at every Lakers home game, courtesy of tickets provided by then owner Bob Short. Short hoped that her attendance would inspire other stars to attend as well. His plan worked. From talk-show host Arsenio Hall to actors such as Leonardo DiCaprio, Denzel Washington, Andy Garcia, and Dyan Cannon, celebrities have regularly shown up at Lakers games ever since. The team's biggest star supporter, however, was actor Jack Nicholson, who had held courtside seats for home games for more than three decades as of 2014. Nicholson was known to holler at referees and hassle fans from opposing teams, but the team appreciated his near-perfect attendance. "He's a real fan," said former Lakers player and coach Pat Riley. "He's not one of these actors that all of sudden gets front-row seats and then they're gone. He's for real. He cares."

tall and 285-pound Andrew Bynum, a promising center. Midway through the season, Phil Jackson returned as head coach. With Bryant scoring an average of 35.4 points per game—including an incredible 81-point game—the Lakers returned to the playoffs in 2006. Although the Suns defeated them in the first round in both 2006 and 2007, Los Angeles looked like it was ready to rebound.

In 2007–08, the Lakers continued to build around Bryant. They traded for dominating forward Pau Gasol, and Bryant responded by giving his best performance ever. He earned his first league MVP award as the Lakers made a return to the Finals against their longtime rivals, the Celtics.

lthough the Lakers lost that series in six games, the team had given notice that it was an NBA power once again. Any doubts about that were erased as Los Angeles rose up to claim its 15th and 16th league championships in 2009 and 2010. Behind Bryant, Gasol, and forward Lamar Odom, the 2008–09 Lakers rolled to a 65-17 record and crushed the Orlando Magic in the Finals. The following year, after adding forward Ron Artest, a defensive specialist, the Lakers delighted the L.A. faithful by beating their archrivals, the Celtics, in the Finals. In the deciding Game 7, the Lakers overcame a 13-point, third-quarter deficit to emerge victorious. Bryant, who was named Finals MVP, considered it the greatest of his five championships. "This one is by far the sweetest, because it's them [the Celtics]," he said. "This was the hardest one by far."

Success did not get any easier. The next year, the Lakers lost to the eventual champions, the Dallas Mavericks, in the Western Conference semifinals, and Jackson retired again afterward. In 2012, Los Angeles hired coach Mike Brown and acquired center Dwight Howard, but its eventual playoff result was the same.

More changes came the following year, as Brown was fired and replaced with offensive-minded coach Mike D'Antoni. "This is a great city to have an up-tempo, exciting game that has a legitimate shot to win a championship," the new coach said. "I can't ask for anything more." Late in the 2012–13 season, Bryant suffered a season-ending Achilles injury. Howard and Gasol helped the Lakers sneak into the playoffs, but their stay was short, as the Spurs knocked them out of the first round in a four-game sweep.

Things only got worse in 2013–14. Howard left for Houston, and aging point guard Steve Nash was sidelined by injury. After plummeting to the bottom of the Western Conference, the struggling Lakers were eliminated from playoff contention by mid-March.

Historically, though, the Los Angeles Lakers have been one of the NBA's most glamorous and triumphant franchises for more than half a century. The team has always set its expectations high—and its fans have come to expect nothing but the greatest performances from the stars who shine brightest on the big stage of the Staples Center.

ALL-STAR AND TWO-TIME MVP GUARD STEVE NASH (#10) JOINED THE LAKERS IN 2012.

INDEX